BITCOIN IS THE FUTURE.

*The Knowleadge you Need to
Dive into Crypto World*

◆ ◆ ◆

Let's start with a quick poll here.

How many of you have used a digital currency like bitcoin at least once?

How many of you own bitcoin at this moment, or any

other cryptocurrency?

Bitcoin -- and the digital currency revolution it has started -- is best demonstrated and experienced, than explained.

It is actually very difficult to explain Bitcoin. I've spent the last five years learning how to explain Bitcoin. That is my full-time job. Unfortunately (or fortunately), developers keep making new stuff which I then have to explain all over again.

For a moment, forget everything you think you know about Bitcoin. Forget everything you've heard about blockchains. Let's start from basics.

In 2011, I heard about Bitcoin for the first time. My reaction was exactly the same as the reaction of everybody else who heard about Bitcoin the first time, including its founder, and that reaction was: "Hah, nerd money! That is probably just for gambling."

Six months later, I heard about Bitcoin again. This time, I read the whitepaper which launched this system. My background in computer science and distributed systems allowed me to see behind the illusion of what I thought Bitcoin was, and it blew my mind.

In my life, I have now had six occasions in which I have become absolutely obsessed with a system of technology to the point of forgetting to eat, forgetting to sleep, and consuming as much knowledge as I possibly can: my first computer when I was ten years old, my first programming language experience, my first modem, my first access to the web, the first time I used a web browser, the first time I downloaded and installed the Linux operating system, and then Bitcoin.

When I discovered it, I spent four months consuming as much as I could, except food. I lost twenty-six pounds on the highly inadvisable diet of obsession. I have not really re-emerged from that, because I keep finding new layers of depth to understand this.

THE REASON IT IS SO FASCINATING?

It isn't what it appears to be at first glance. Bitcoin isn't just money. The blockchain isn't a system of currency. It is a platform of trust. It is not a company, it is not a product, it is not a service that you sign up for. It is not just a currency. Currency is the first application. It is the concept of decentralization applied to the human communication of value.

What is money?

As INQ told us, it is an illusion. It is imaginary. The reason we don't grasp that is because money is so deeply embedded in our civilization. Money is one of the oldest technologies that humanity has. It precedes writing.

How do we know that?

The very first samples of writing we have are spreadsheets tallies and ledgers of debts owed, of money pre-existed that writing. You might even speculate that money had an oral tradition until it needed to invent a written tradition, and so a system of writing was created for it.

In the history of money that spans tens of thousands

of years, there have been maybe five major changes. From pure barter exchange to the first abstraction of value, shells, feathers, beads, nuts, stones, and precious metals. Then paper money, and plastic money, and now network money.

Bitcoin introduces a platform on which you can run currency as an application, a network without any central points of control, a system that is decentralized like the internet itself. It is not money "for" the internet but the internet "of" money.

And what is money?

Money is a language, a linguistic abstraction, that we use to communicate value to each other. Money simply allows us to express value which may have economic consequences, but it also has other consequences. We use money to express and create social bonds, relationships, associations, and organisations.

THE FIRST COMPLETELY DECENTRALIZED SYSTEM OF MONEY

Bitcoin is the first system of money that is not controlled by any single entity, that is completely decentralized. It introduces the very same effects that the internet brought to communication. If money is speech, if money is a language, and you disconnect it from all other media to make it pure speech, pure content, an internet content type, a protocol designation, money over IP. It completely separates it from all previous notions of nations, sovereign issuers, institutions that control. We transition from institution-based money to a network-based money.

Of course, everyone will welcome this with open arms. Not a chance!

What do you think people said the first time someone was presented with a gold depository certificate, instead of a gold coin? They said: "Hah, that's not money! Go away." What do you think happened in 1950 when someone showed up at a motel, presented their diners' club membership card, and said, "I'll pay with this piece of paper." "That's not money. Go away!" Now we are on the verge of a new transformation of money, of creating the first completely global, borderless, decentralized, and open form of money. Money where you can build applications because it is programmable. You don't need to ask for anyone's permission to launch an application any more than you need to ask for permission to launch an application on the internet. The only requirement to have a successful application on the 'internet of money' is two interested participants. That is your minimum market segment and you have an application. A million applications will flourish.

THE UPCOMING INNOVATION EXPLOSION

When you push innovation to the edges of the network, when you remove the requirement for permission, what happens?

An exponential explosion of innovation in applications that could not be built on the old systems of money, because those systems required permission, required a significantly large market segment, required adoption by many in order to be available at all. Now, none of those requirements exist. Anyone in the world can download an application or use even a feature phone with text messaging, and immediately acquire the same powers that institutions of banking have today.

When I say anyone, that is only scratching the surface. Not only does Bitcoin's currency not recognize borders, it also does not recognize people. It doesn't matter if you are a person, a refrigerator, or a self-driving car.

Throughout the history of money, ownership of currency required personhood, either as an individual or an association of individuals in a corporation. Bitcoin can be owned by machines, by software agents. Machines can pay each other. And that is not just about economic activity. It is the basis for a market-based security system. It is the basis for creating bonds of authentication between devices. It is the basis for new applications that have never been done before.

Bitcoin and blockchain technology unifies the various systems of money. Today we have systems of money for small payments and systems of money for large payments. We have systems of money for payments between individuals, payments between companies, and for payments between governments.

Does that remind you of something?

That is how communication used to be before the internet. We had systems of communication for pictures, systems of communication for letters, for short distances and long distances. The internet came and unified all of those. 'The Internet of Money' creates a single network which can do a micro-transaction to a giga-transaction (in terms of the amount of bitcoin), in seconds, anywhere in the world, for any participant without permission.

But if you just look at the application of money, you are missing the point. You can take the language, the building blocks of this platform, and use it to construct other languages that communicate value: tokens, reward points, and brand loyalty coins. Today, there are over a thousand digital currencies using the design pattern, the recipe, of Bitcoin. Most of them are junk, some of them are not.

Over the next decade, we will see tens of thousands,

and then hundreds of thousands, of coins. Some will have economic use; some will simply be expressions of loyalty and affiliation. They may represent items in the physical world, such as the title for a house or the key for a car, that can be transferred from one owner to another. Five seconds later, that new owner can step into the car and drive away, because the car can validate the standard of ownership.

We cannot yet imagine what applications we will build around this. One of the interesting things we have observed is that money arises out of the social constructs of homo sapiens spontaneously, and even arises in primates. You can teach monkeys about money. You can teach dolphins about money. You can teach grey parrots money. They will learn how to exchange abstract tokens for food and then use them to build social relationships. They will also invent strong-arm robbery: beat up the other monkey, take away its pebbles, eat the bananas.

We see that same thing happen in children. Toddlers invent money in Kindergarten. Wooden blocks, rubber bands, Pokemon cards and other little tokens that are abstractions of value. They exchange to strengthen social bonds, to express loyalty and friendship, to learn about sharing. Children will be building currencies, only this time these currencies could be global, unforgeable, and scalable. A few years from now, Maria will be launching MariaCoin in her kindergarten to compete against JoeyCoin. It won't really matter to anyone. Until, of course, Justin Bieber launches Bieber-Coin and it happens to surpass the market capitalization of thirty nations on this planet. We will all write horrified opinion editorials about how the world is going to hell.

INNOVATION: BANKING VS BITCOIN

What is happening with this technology is astonishingly deep; for some companies in this room, it is a bit scary. Banking has never been the most innovative sector in the world. There is a very careful balance between innovation and the conservative fiduciary duty that exists in banking, that must exist when you control other people's money. Yet with Bitcoin, you don't control other people's money. In Bitcoin, I control my money. I have complete authority over my bitcoin. It cannot be seized, frozen, or censored. My transactions cannot be intercepted, cannot be stopped. I can do so with anonymity, and so can anyone else within five minutes of downloading a wallet application.

Money has changed forever. Banking has changed forever.

The idea that you can proceed in the industries of money and commerce, and maintain the same conservative attitude that has existed for centuries, ever since merchants in Venice and Amsterdam issued depository certificates and providing banking services. That is gone, that is gone! You cannot operate closed systems that have borders, that require permission to join, that limit innovation, that is controlled by the most conservative tendencies within your organization. Now you are competing with a technology that enables exponential growth, innovation at the edges, without permission, by anyone in the world. It is not about anyone in this room.

Why?

We represent the privileged elite. I can open an online brokerage account and be trading on the Tokyo stock market within twelve hours, in yen. That is a privilege that I have. About 1.5 billion people also have that privilege. The other six billion people can operate mainly in one currency and perhaps have basic banking services. Four billion people are significantly underbanked. An astonishing 2.5 billion people are unbanked. They will leapfrog the old system of banking. They will never have a relationship with a bank. Every single child born today will never have a bank account. They will have a banking app. A bank app that doesn't just give them an account, but that makes them a banker, an international banker in an app. They will not be permitted to open a bank account until they are at least sixteen years old. By that time, I hope they will have at least six years of experience with digital currencies. I would like to watch them walk into a bank branch, where someone tries to explain to them what "three to five business days" means. It is highly likely the children born today will never get a driving license because they'll have self-driving cars. But they may also never use paper money. By the time they reach an age where they really start using money, there is no paper money. It will seem as anachronistic as a fax machine, or horse-and-buggy, seems to us.

Exponential innovation on a global basis, giving access to the other six billion who have enormous need. This system offers them a solution. It is not quite ready yet. It is nascent, complex, and impossible to use for most people.

In 1989, I sent my first email. I needed to first compile a version of the Unix mail program using a C compiler and Unix command line skills. I typed out my email, which was transmitted across the great internet in an astonishingly fast three days. Exactly twenty years later, my mother replicated that experience with a swipe of her finger. Today, bitcoin -- and all of the other currencies built on that recipe -- are at the same development level that the internet was at in 1991.

Now we have the internet, so exponential growth has already started. Innovation is happening at an astonishing rate. I spend every single day, full-time, trying to keep up with Bitcoin. Just one currency, and it is almost impossible to keep up. Do not underestimate this. Do not listen to the people who tell you that bitcoin is just for pornographers, terrorists, drug dealers, and gamblers. Remember that they said the exact same things about the internet. When you give it to two or three billion people, they are not interested in those things the media warned about. They are interested in sharing cat videos. Now we have an internet of a billion cat videos. When you take digital currency mainstream and give it to the four billion people who have been isolated from international finance and commerce, you give them control of their money against despotic governments and corrupt banks that are stealing from them. You give them the opportunity to control their future, the opportunity to transact with everyone in the world, to own title on their property in a fully transferable digital token that could be recognized everywhere. They can have control over their finances that cannot be seized, frozen, or censored. They will buy food, healthcare, sanitation, education, and shelter, because that is what humans do. They will not be denied this technology. Do not underestimate where this is going.

'The internet of money' was launched on January 3rd, 2009. It is coming. It is coming faster than you can imagine. It is deeper than you can fathom, more sophisticated than you will immediately understand. It will take years of study just to see all of the implications. It is a gift to the entire world. It represents the sixth greatest innovation in money, the most ancient technology of our civilization.

WHAT DETERMINES THE BUYING POWER OF THE CURRENCY?

How does it stabilize and what's required to stabilize it, so if I would buy some Bitcoins, who can manipulate the value of that? Mhm, everyone. The buying power of Bitcoin is determined in exactly the same way that the buying power of the euro, the British sterling, the Japanese yen, or the US Dollar is determined through market forces of supply and demand in international liquid markets that operate around the clock. One of the fundamental differences is that bitcoin trading never ceases. Has been going continuously for seven years the network never stops. Every ten minutes Bitcoins heart beats and transactions are processed, the exchanges never close. There is no closing price for Bitcoin. It is a rolling average and in that trading a market capitalization of approximately twelve billion dollars is now traded internationally. What is twelve billion dollars for a global currency? It's a guppy, swimming in shark-infested waters and every trader, every whale goes in there and just kicks that price around. So right now the experience of living on Bitcoin which I have been doing full-time for more than three years is a roller coaster. It's an absolute roller coaster. I've seen shifts of 20 or 30 percent in a day and yet, if you look at the long-term trend, volume goes up, transactions go up, and volatility keeps dropping. And the beauty of it is, I can't sell that to an American. I can't sell that to a Brit. I don't need to sell it to an Argentinean. I don't need to sell it to a Brazilian. I don't need to sell it to a Venezuelan.

I went to a conference and an Argentinian told me I'm not worried about volatility, our currency has volatility like this. Bitcoin has volatility like this. I'd rather be going in that direction. And you don't need to tell them why. Their government through people out of airplanes not more than 35 years ago for disagreeing. They already know why the separation of state and money is a good idea. And so volatility is relative.

WHAY ABOUT HACKING RISKS?

The steering wheel was not invented until 30 years after the automobile was introduced. Why?

Because the first automobiles had two leather straps that you pulled left or right to move the car, to steer the car. They used horse reins to steer cars. That's called skeuomorphic design. It means keeping a shadow of the former past in your new system, failing to see the new dimension and replicating the past.

Here's a currency that is not centralized where your money is your money. Your keys, your money. Not your keys, not your money. So, what is the first thing we do with this new system? We build centralized institutional's of custodial control that take other peoples money and hold it for them. Well, guess what? The entire history of banking, the entire system of regulation and oversight is based on the simple centuries-old understanding that when somebody else holds your money, chances are they're going to run away with it. And the entire system of regulation is designed to prevent that and yet it still happens all the time. In hedge funds, in banks, in national currencies, all the time. And so of course, if you replicate custodial accounts, exchanges that take other people's Bitcoin and concentrate it It happens again, even worse because there are no oversight and regulations in most of these spaces.

The answer is really simple. Stop centralizing the decentralized currency. Stop trying to replicate the banking past in the future of money. And the important thing to realize is that security in Bitcoin is an emergent property that exists because of the decentralization of control and power. If I want to hack a million customers Bitcoin, And they're holding their keys, I have to hack a million customers. If they all give their keys to one person or one organization, then we've got a honeypot. A honeypot that attracts the attention of every hacker on the planet. And notice what's happened. Over seven years and with a market capitalization of twelve billion dollars, Bitcoin is the largest cryptographic deployment in the world, the largest public key infrastructure in the world, the largest security honeypot in the world and it is not secure because it doesn't get attacked. It is secure because it generates immunity by being attacked all the time, 24 hours a day by the most sophisticated attackers this planet has. And if you in that environment set up a centralized custodial exchange using PHP and MySQL and you park a 150 million dollar Honeypot in there, you're inviting the sharks.

Bitcoin banks get hacked, Bitcoin exchanges get hacked, Bitcoin has not been hacked and cannot be hacked because there is no point of control that you can apply pressure on. It's completely decentralized.

Where does the supply of Bitcoin come from and are you sure the market doesn't get oversupplied?

The supply of Bitcoin is determined algorithmically based on a geometrically declining supply function, meaning that, in the beginning every 10 minutes, 50 new Bitcoin are created, so every block, the heartbeat, 10 minutes, created 50 new Bitcoin. This Bitcoin is used as a reward in a game theory based security model that ensures that every transaction is independently validated by completely anonymous actors who have to stake electricity as a guarantee of the security work they've done and if they succeed in doing the security work validating transactions correctly, they earn as a reward based on a probabilistic return. That reward, 50 Bitcoin every 10 minutes. That's how currency is introduced into the economy.

Every four years it gets cut in half. 50 to 25 in November of 2012. And this year in July, this past July, we had our second having event which was celebrated with birthday parties all over the world and Bitcoins reward went from 25 to 12.5 Bitcoin.

As a system, it's designed to have a monetary policy that is purposely deflationary and simulates the issuance of precious metals. It gets harder and harder and harder to mine gold at greater and greater and greater cost. And Bitcoin is the same. The idea being that less and less is issued over time. If you follow that geometric curve, at some point, you reach the end. In the year 2141 Bitcoin is no longer issued. 21 million coins is the asymptotic cap. It will never reach 21 million coins.

That is part of the protocol, it is an unchangeable part of the protocol and it is a rule enforced by every system that participates in the Bitcoin network. It is meant to be sound money but it's not the only monetary policy that exists. There are several other currencies that implement different monetary policies.

The idea is really for Bitcoin to serve as a very very solid reserve currency for many other things. What do you have to give to companies here who are from non-financial institutions about how they should take tactical steps to think about experimenting with the blockchain in terms of storing value? I think understanding that it's not just currency, understanding that it is a platform for trust. Understanding that it can be used as a historical record of truths that can register information that it can be used to create all kinds of tokens that can be exchanged between your customers, your suppliers, your manufacturers, that it can also be used simply as a currency for any cross-border transactions import/export activities, remittances based flows, paying associates and affiliates. All of the things that today are expensive, slow, and difficult become cheap, fast, and easy when you use one of these digital currencies. But It's still early. For now, learning about it.

Here's the one important thing you must understand. You will hear a lot about blockchain and most of what you hear about blockchain is not The Internet of Money. It is The Intranet of Money. The Intranet is where you run FrontPage and Outlook and antiquated software in a closed little enclave of your corporate back waters with stale content and boring apps. And in the end, it's full of viruses anyway because you can't keep it secure. Blockchain that is not open, that is not public, that is not borderless that is not open for innovation is not what we're talking about here. And that's a really important distinction. It may be useful if you want to run a clearing house between three banks, maybe. But it's not The Internet of Money.

INVESTING

At this point you might be willing to invest in bitcoin, so that's why here i present a series of MUST KNOWs before you dive into the fascinating cryptocurrency world.

Buying Bitcoin is getting easier by the day and the legitimacy of the exchanges and wallets is growing as well but can seem complicated if you don't break it down into steps.

While it is nearly impossible for Bitcoin itself to be hacked, it is possible for your wallet or exchange account to be compromised. This is why practicing proper storage and security measures is imperative.

Investing or trading Bitcoin only requires an account on an exchange, though further safe storage practices are recommended.

BEFORE YOU BEGIN

There are several things that every aspiring Bitcoin investor needs. A cryptocurrency exchange account, personal identification documents if you are using a Know Your Customer (KYC) platform, a secure connection to the Internet, and a method of payment. It is also recommended that you have your own personal wallet outside of the exchange account. Valid methods of payment using this path include bank accounts, debit cards, and credit cards. It is also possible to get Bitcoin at specialized ATMs and via P2P exchanges. However, be aware that Bitcoin ATMs were increasingly requiring government-issued IDs as of early 2020.

To buy bitcoin you need a digital wallet, personal identifying documents, a secure internet connection, a cryptocurrency exchange, and a form of payment.

Privacy and security are important issues for Bitcoin investors.

Even though there are no physical Bitcoins, it is usually a bad idea to brag about large holdings. Anyone who gains the private key to a public address on the Bitcoin blockchain can authorize transactions. While it is obvious that the private key should be kept secret, criminals may attempt to steal private keys if they learn of large holdings. Be aware that anyone can see the balance of a public address that you use. That makes it a good idea to keep significant investments at public addresses that are not directly connected to ones that are used for transactions.

Anyone can view a history of transactions made on the blockchain, even you. But while transactions are publicly recorded on the blockchain, identifying user information is not. On the Bitcoin blockchain, only a user's public key appears next to a transaction—making transactions confidential but not anonymous. In a sense, Bitcoin transactions are more transparent and traceable than cash, but Bitcoin can be used anonymously.

That is an important distinction. International researchers and the FBI have claimed that they can track transactions made on the Bitcoin blockchain to users' other online accounts, including their digital wallets.

For example, if someone creates an account on Coinbase they must provide their identification. Now, when that person purchases Bitcoin it is tied to their name. If they send it to another wallet it can still be traced back to the Coinbase purchase which was connected to the account holder's identity. This should not concern most investors because Bitcoin is legal in the U.S. and most other developed countries.

STEP ONE: CHOOSE AN EXCHANGE

Signing up for a cryptocurrency exchange will allow you to buy, sell, and hold cryptocurrency. It is generally best practice to use an exchange that allows its users to also withdrawal their crypto to their own personal wallet for safer keeping. There are many exchanges and brokerage platforms that do not allow this. For those looking to consistently trade Bitcoin or other cryptocurrencies, this feature may not matter.

There are many types of cryptocurrency exchanges that exist. With the ethos of Bitcoin being decentralization and individual sovereignty, some exchanges allow users to remain anonymous and do not require users to enter personal information. Exchanges that allow this operate autonomously and are typically decentralized which means there is no central point of control. In other words, there is no CEO and no person or group for any regulatory body to pursue should it have concerns over illegal activity taking place.

While these types of systems do have the potential to be used for nefarious activities, they also provide services to the unbanked world. People like this may include refugees or those living in countries where there is little to no government or banking infrastructure to provide a state identification required for a bank or investment account. Some believe the good in these services outweigh the potential for illegal use as unbanked people now have a means of storing wealth and can use it to climb out of poverty.

Right now, the most commonly used type of exchanges are not decentralized and do require KYC. In the United States, these exchanges include Coinbase, Kraken, Gemini, and Binance U.S., to name a few. Each of these exchanges has grown significantly in the number of features they offer. Coinbase, Kraken, and Gemini offer Bitcoin and a growing number of altcoins. These three are probably the easiest on-ramp to crypto in the entire industry. Binance caters to a more advanced trader, offering more serious trading functionality and numerous altcoins to choose from.

An important thing to note when creating a cryptocurrency exchange account is to use safe internet practices. This includes using two-factor authentication and using a password that is unique and long, including a variety of lowercase letters, capitalized letters, special characters, and numbers.

STEP TWO: CONNECT YOUR EXCHANGE TO A PAYMENT OPTION

Once you have chosen an exchange, you now need to gather your personal documents. Depending on the exchange, these may include pictures of a driver's license, social security number, as well as information about your employer and source of funds. The information you may need can depend on the region you live in and the laws within it. The process is largely the same as setting up a typical brokerage account.

By linking a bank account to your wallet, you can buy and sell bitcoin and deposit that money directly into your account.

After the exchange has ensured your identity and legitimacy you may now connect a payment option. With the exchanges listed above, you can connect your bank account directly or you can connect a debit or credit card. While you can use a credit card to purchase cryptocurrency, it is generally something that should be avoided due to the volatility that cryptocurrencies can experience.

While Bitcoin is legal in the United States, some banks

do not take too kindly to the idea and may question or even stop deposits to crypto-related sites or exchanges. While most banks do allow these deposits, it is a good idea to check to make sure that your bank allows deposits at your chosen exchange.

There are varying fees for deposits via a bank account, debit, or credit card. Coinbase, for example, which is a solid exchange for beginners, has a 1.49% fee for bank accounts and a 3.99% fee for debit and credit cards. It is important to research the fees associated with each payment option to help choose an exchange or to choose which payment option works best for you.

STEP THREE: PLACE AN ORDER

Once you have chosen an exchange and connected a payment option you can now buy Bitcoin and other cryptocurrencies. Over recent years cryptocurrency and their exchanges have slowly become more mainstream. Exchanges have grown significantly in terms of liquidity and their breadth of features. What was once thought of as a scam or questionable has developed into something that could be considered trustworthy and legitimate.

Now, cryptocurrency exchanges have gotten to a point where they have nearly the same level of features as their stock brokerage counterparts. Once you have found an exchange and connected a payment method you are ready to go.

Crypto exchanges today offer a number of order types and ways to invest. Almost all crypto exchanges offer both market and limit orders and some also offer stop-loss orders. Of the exchanges mentioned above, Kraken offers the most order types. Kraken allows for market, limit, stop-loss, stop-limit, and take-profit limit orders.

Aside from a variety of order types, exchanges also offer ways to set up recurring investments allowing clients to dollar cost average into their investments of choice. Coinbase, for example, lets users set recurring purchases for every day, week, or month. Getting an account on an exchange is really all you need to do to be able to buy Bitcoin or other cryptocurrencies, but there are some other steps to consider for more safety and security.

STEP FOUR: SAFE STORAGE

Bitcoin and cryptocurrency wallets are a place to store digital assets more securely. Having your crypto outside of the exchange and in your personal wallet ensures that only you have control over the private key to your funds. It also gives you the ability to store funds away from an exchange and avoid the risk of your exchange getting hacked and losing your funds.

While most exchanges offer wallets for their users, security is not their primary business. We generally do not recommend using an exchange wallet for large or long-term cryptocurrency holdings.

Some wallets have more features than others. Some are Bitcoin only and some offer the ability to store numerous types of altcoins. Some wallets also offer the ability to swap one token for another.

When it comes to choosing a Bitcoin wallet, you have a number of options. The first thing that you will need to understand about crypto wallets is the concept of hot wallets (online wallets) and cold wallets (paper or hardware wallets).

Hot Wallets

Online wallets are also known as "hot" wallets. Hot wallets are wallets that run on internet-connected devices like computers, phones, or tablets. This can create vulnerability because these wallets generate the private keys to your coins on these internet-connected devices. While a hot wallet can be very convenient in the way you are able to access and make transactions with your assets quickly, storing your private key on an internet-connected device makes it more susceptible to a hack.

This may sound far-fetched, but people who are not using enough security when using these hot wallets can have their funds stolen. This is not an infrequent occurrence and it can happen in a number of ways. As an example, boasting on a public forum like Reddit about how much Bitcoin you hold while you are using little to no security and storing it in a hot wallet would not be wise. That said, these wallets can be made to be secure so long as precautions are taken. Strong passwords, two-factor authentication, and safe internet browsing should be considered minimum requirements.

These wallets are best used for small amounts of cryptocurrency or cryptocurrency that you are actively trading on an exchange. You could liken a hot wallet to a checking account. Conventional financial wisdom would say to hold only spending money in a checking account while the bulk of your money is in savings accounts or other investment accounts. The same could be said for hot wallets. Hot wallets encompass mobile, desktop, web, and exchange account custody wallets.

As mentioned previously, exchange wallets are custodial accounts provided by the exchange. The user of this wallet type is not the holder of the private key to the cryptocurrency that is held in this wallet. If an event were to occur where the exchange is hacked or your account becomes compromised, your funds would be lost. The phrase "not your key, not your coin" is a heavily repeated concept within cryptocurrency forums and communities.

Cold Wallets

The simplest description of a cold wallet is a wallet that is not connected to the internet and therefore stands at a far lesser risk of being compromised. These wallets can also be referred to as offline wallets or hardware wallets.

These wallets store a user's private key on something that is not connected to the internet and can come with software that works in parallel so that the user can view their portfolio without putting their private key at risk.

Perhaps the most secure way to store cryptocurrency offline is via a paper wallet. A paper wallet is a wallet that you can generate off of certain websites. It then produces both public and private keys that you print out on a piece of paper. The ability to access cryptocurrency in these addresses is only possible if you have that piece of paper with the private key. Many people laminate these paper wallets and store them in safety deposit boxes at their bank or even in a safe in their home. These wallets are meant for high security and long-term investments because you cannot quickly sell or trade Bitcoin stored this way.

A more commonly used type of cold wallet is a hardware wallet. A hardware wallet is typically a USB drive device that stores a user's private keys securely offline. This has serious advantages over hot wallets as it is unaffected by viruses that could be on one's computer. With hardware wallets, private keys never come in contact with your network-connected computer or potentially vulnerable software. These devices are also typically open source, allowing the community to determine its safety through code audits rather than a company declaring that it is safe to use.

Cold wallets are the most secure way to store your Bitcoin or other cryptocurrencies. For the most part, however, they require a bit more knowledge to set up.

A good way to set up your wallets is to have three things: an exchange account to buy and sell, a hot wallet to hold small to medium amounts of crypto you wish to trade or sell, and a cold hardware wallet to store larger holdings for long-term durations.

ALTERNATE WAYS OF BUYING BITCOIN

While exchanges like Coinbase or Binance remain some of the most popular ways of purchasing Bitcoin, it is not the only method. Below are some additional processes Bitcoin owners utilize.

Bitcoin ATMs

Bitcoin ATMs act like in-person Bitcoin exchanges. Individuals can insert cash into the machine and use it to purchase Bitcoin that is then transferred to a secure digital wallet. Bitcoin ATMs have become increasingly popular in recent years; Coin ATM Radar can help to track down the closest machines.

P2P Exchanges

Unlike decentralized exchanges, which match up buyers and sellers anonymously and facilitate all aspects of the transaction, there are some peer-to-peer (P2P) exchange services that provide a more direct connection between users. Local Bitcoins is an example of such an exchange. After creating an account, users can post requests to buy or sell Bitcoin, including information about payment methods and price. Users then browse through listings of buy and sell offers, choosing those trade partners with whom they wish to transact.

Local Bitcoins facilitates some of the aspects of the trade. While P2P exchanges do not offer the same anonymity as decentralized exchanges, they allow users the opportunity to shop around for the best deal. Many of these exchanges also provide rating systems so that users have a way to evaluate potential trade partners before transacting.

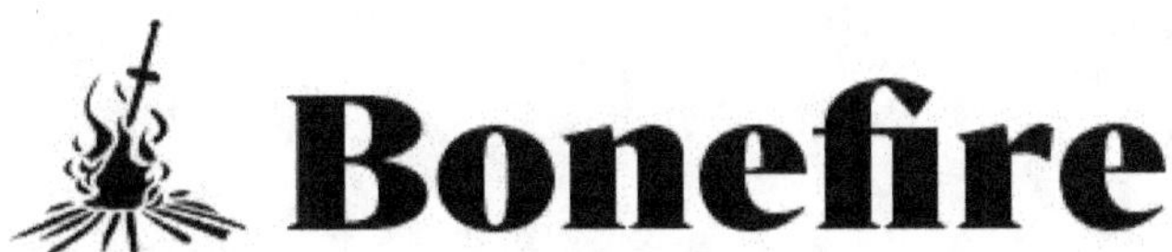

Thank you for trusting Bonefire Editorial.

This work is the product of the dedication and commitment of those great men and women who, through their art, have made our world a more interesting and vibrant place.

Their legacy still burns among us through their magical writing. We extend to them our sincerest gratitude.

To read is to hear with the eyes those who are long gone.

www.ingramcontent.com/pod-product-compliance
Lightning Source LLC
Chambersburg PA
CBHW060925130726
48001CB00006B/2420